PAINTING BY THE POST-IMPRESSIONISTS

by Alfred Werner

McGRAW-HILL BOOK COMPANY

New York   Toronto   London

For a list of other titles in this series, see page 48

THE POST-IMPRESSIONISTS

Movements in modern art have often received their names from hostile critics, like the one who coined the term "Impressionists" in 1874, for the revolutionaries associated with Monet, Pissarro, Sisley; or another who in 1905 called Matisse and his gang "Wild Beasts" (Fauves).

The term "Post-Impressionism," however, was created by a British painter and critic, Roger Fry (1866–1934), whose own pictures are now forgotten. The phrase had an unusual origin. In France, Fry had seen and admired paintings by Manet, Cézanne, Gauguin, Van Gogh, Seurat, Matisse, Picasso and others who were either totally unknown or ignored in England. He gathered together works of these French masters for two group shows at the Grafton Galleries in London, intending to dazzle his conservative compatriots. The term "Post-Impressionists" was selected as the name for the shows; it was not a felicitous choice, for it simply implied that these men came after the Impressionists. Even chronologically this was not quite correct, for Manet actually antedated the Impressionists and, in his early works at least, blended Romanticism and Realism. Matisse (aged forty-one) and

Picasso (aged twenty-nine), on the other hand, were by 1910 already the leaders of independent schools, Fauvism and Cubism, that had aims and principles entirely of their own.

Nevertheless, the faulty and inadequate term "Post-Impressionism" continues to be used by art historians as a name for the fine, bold pictures, executed with little regard for photographic truth between about 1886, when Impressionism began to decline, and about 1905, when the far more aggressive "Wild Beasts" or Fauves made their appearance. In recent decades, the cast of characters to be covered by this term has often been cut down considerably to the "Holy Trinity" (Cézanne, Gauguin and Van Gogh); the Neo-Impressionist Seurat; Toulouse-Lautrec; the "Nabis" Bonnard and Vuillard, also called Intimists; and such extraordinary men as Redon, Ensor, and the "customs inspector" Rousseau who do not quite fit into any other category.

By the end of 1910 only Redon and the much younger Ensor, Bonnard and Vuillard were still alive and active. Before the Grafton Galleries shows, works of these artists had never been united under one roof. Yet, though they were not linked by any real organization, as had existed with the Impressionists, they have much in common beyond the name so arbitrarily chosen for them. In the catalogue prefaces to the second Post-Impressionist show (London, 1912), Fry and his associate Clive Bell tried to demonstrate the common denominator that justified the grouping of these men and defended them against hostile accusations. It was not true that all of them were unskilled; it was true of only one, the untrained Henri Rousseau:

"His pretensions to paint made him the butt of a great deal of ironic wit, but scarcely anyone now would deny the authentic quality of his inspiration or the certainty of his imaginative convictions. Here then is one case where want of skill and knowledge do not completely obscure, though they may mar, expression."

Fry also defended the group against accusations of insincerity and extravagance that, he explained, arose from the pub-

Figure 1. Paul Signac:
The Port of Marseilles.
Louvre, Paris

lic's misunderstanding of their aims. These artists, he wrote, did not think that the descriptive imitation of natural forms was the aim of painting:

"... they do not seek to give what can, after all, be but a pale reflex of actual appearance, but to arouse the conviction of a new and definite reality. They do not seek to imitate form, but to create form; not to imitate life, but to find an [artistic] equivalent for life. By that I mean that they wish to make images which by the clearness of their logical structure, and by their closely-knit unity of texture, shall appeal to our disinterested and contemplative imagination with something of the same vividness as the things of actual life appeal to our practical activities."

Clive Bell, too, expressed himself on the subject in sentences that after half a century are still useful to the understanding of all art:

"We have ceased to ask, 'What does this painting represent?' and ask instead, 'What does it make us feel?' We expect a work of art to have more in common with a piece of music than with a colored photograph.

"In what way then does the Post-Impressionist distinguish himself from other painters? Primarily insofar as he simplifies, omits details, that is to say, to concentrate on something more important — on the *significance of form*" (the italics are mine).

Fry might have called his group the anti-Impressionists, even though several of the men whose works he gathered had originally exhibited with the Impressionists, especially Cézanne, Redon, Gauguin and Seurat, while all the others, with the exception of "Primitive" Rousseau, had passed through a longer or shorter Impressionist phase (the humble Cézanne and even the far from humble Gauguin to the end of their days gratefully acknowledged their debt to Pissarro). In the 1880's these men had already begun to weary of Impressionism; although it had appeared as a revolutionary movement, in reality it only brought

Figure 2. Paul Signac:
Les Alyscamps, Arles.

Collection, The Museum
of Modern Art, New York
Acquired through the
Lillie P. Bliss Bequest

6

to a climax the Renaissance ideal of the most accurate representation of nature. In his eagerness to record as precisely as possible the way objects actually appeared in the surrounding light, Monet ended by dissolving the façade of Rouen Cathedral into thin atmospheric mists. "Monet is only an eye," Cézanne remarked (though he added, in admiration, "But what an eye!"). The young critic, Felix Fénéon, a friend of Seurat and Signac, even dared to accuse the old and successful Monet of "brilliant vulgarity!" Paul Signac who, with the more important Georges Seurat, developed the art and theory of "Neo-Impressionism," made perfectly clear the difference between the Impressionist and himself. The former, devoid of theory, paints the way "a bird sings." The Neo-Impressionist, we are informed, approaches his motif with reason, studying the phenomena of light in an orderly, rational manner and trying to create beauty by means of harmony. The Impressionists had "a technique depending on instinct and the inspiration of the moment"; their heirs and successors, by contrast, boasted of a "methodical and scientific technique." Signac charged that the Impressionist painter reduced the brilliance of his colors by a "muddy mixture of pigments," injuring his work "by an intermittent and irregular application of the laws governing color." He and Seurat had a different approach:

"By the elimination of all muddy mixtures, by the exclusive use of the optical mixture of pure colors, by a methodical divisionism and a strict observation of the scientific theory of colors, the Neo-impressionist insures a maximum of luminosity, of color intensity, and of harmony — a result that has never yet been obtained."

This was written in 1899, years before the term "Post-Impressionist" was coined and years after the split within the Impressionist camp. While it was meant to apply only to the long-deceased Seurat, to Signac himself, and to a few others who joined the Neo-Impressionists (also called "Pointillists" and

"Divisionists"), luminosity, color intensity and harmony were goals of those whose pictures appear in this book, though they did not use the same methods. What they had in common was an abhorrence of submitting to nature's whims or accidents as Monet had done, and a search for the very form and structure that the Impressionists had lost in a veil of shimmering color. Though all of these artists were born in the last century, and the majority of them had ended their careers by the first World War, their insistence upon what Clive Bell later called "significant form" was to have an enormous impact upon artists born after 1900.

The end of Impressionism and the beginning of a new era was marked by two events: in 1884 a new Societé des Artistes Indépendants arranged an exhibition of their works; they included Odilon Redon, aged forty-four, Georges Seurat, aged twenty-five, Paul Signac, who was only twenty-one, and a few others of less importance. Two years later, these three also participated in the eighth Impressionist group show, not knowing that this would be the last Impressionist show, or that leadership in the plastic arts was about to fall to them. For in 1886, some of the men who had been most active at the height of the Impressionist movement, especially Cézanne, Monet, Renoir, and Sisley, were no longer participating, and Degas had sent in only a few pastels. The veteran of all Impressionist shows, Camille Pissarro, who had played an enormous role from the very start of the group, submitted many paintings and pastels, but they were considerably influenced by Seurat's technique of painting in tiny dots of pure color. In lieu of the missing pure Impressionists, now for the first time the keynote was struck by such "Post-Impressionists" as Gauguin, Redon, Signac, and Seurat.

Despite his flirtation with Neo-Impressionism, Pissarro does not belong in an account of the Post-Impressionist story, for he soon abandoned Seurat's theory. Degas is sometimes classed with the Post-Impressionists, yet he stands apart from every school. Though he participated in seven of the eight Impressionist group shows, he never favored outdoor painting. Like Seurat and his friends, rather than surrender himself to nature he insisted upon building a work of art mentally. But he had no direct contact with them, and in the period upon which attention is focused in this book, he was a half-blind recluse, producing little other than an occasional pastel or a piece of sculpture.

It is another recluse, and one who was an even rarer sight in Parisian art circles than the highly unsociable Degas, who must be discussed before the other three major figures (chronologically, Gauguin, Van Gogh, and Seurat) in any story of Post-Impressionism. Cézanne, born in Aix in Southern France in 1839, was a silent participant whenever the Impressionists gathered around a café table. He exhibited with them twice and was usually counted a minor member of the school, perhaps the least gifted one. Yet before meeting Pissarro he had created thickly-painted romantic fancies so curiously violent and often erotic that it is difficult to associate them with the name of Cézanne. At a certain point, around 1883, having returned from Paris to the quiet of Aix, he started to evolve a new style based on architectural solidity rather than on the Impressionists' dissolution of nature into chromatic vibrancies.

He became more and more eager to grasp the secret organization of things, the structure beneath the appearance, the "bones of nature." Moreover, he knew what most good painters have always known, that it is the painter's task to represent, not to reproduce, nature. As a representer, he was no longer nature's slave; he could eliminate nonessentials, ignore haphazard relationships of forms, and arbitrarily construct pictures out of elements, as an architect builds a house, instead of yielding to accident and chaos as presumably the Impressionists had done. Cézanne gradually abandoned light and shade, as well as atmospheric perspective, in order to suggest the third dimension by a rhythmic succession of different color planes. But Cézanne's space is a deliberately controlled arrangement where, instead of accentuating the visually penetrative backward movement of traditional painting, he creates a forward motion for the painting as a whole. This is accomplished by relating the forms and the tonalities of the background to those of the foreground. Nature is expressed by Cézanne as a kind of tension and it is this "sensation" that he is constantly trying to realize.

Figure 3. Paul Cézanne:
Pines and Rocks.

Collection, The Museum
of Modern Art, New York.
Lillie P. Bliss Collection

A creative artist uses his motif for a point of departure. He "distorts" whatever in nature does not fit his concept of beauty. La Montagne Sainte-Victoire near Aix really has none of the grandeur and monumentality Cézanne bestowed upon it. He painted this not particularly impressive small mountain more than sixty times, translating its aesthetic possibilities into his own pictorial idiom. In the interest of relating foreground to background, he has done such things as relate the tree in the right foreground to the mountains in the distance by curving the branches across them until they practically touch those of the tree in the left foreground.

The very ordinary card-players he chose to portray were transfigured into solid forms of austere firmness with the strength of archaic sculpture. All of the objects in the picture are somehow related to the picture frame so that here also we find the artist tensing up his space and moving it forward. In his still lifes of fruit, bottles and glasses, the objects are arranged to achieve a complete synthesis of forms, even if they had to be flattened out or given an alien hue; this procedure was the source of complaints that Cézanne could not master the rudiments of accurate drawing and painting.

A painter does not work to please critics, nor even to instruct his colleagues. But Cézanne, in a letter to a younger artist, did advise the study of geometric forms, an interpretation of nature in terms of the cylinder, the sphere, and the cone. The Cubists (Picasso, Braque, and their associates) certainly interpreted this dictum as an encouragement to move ahead even further in their development of a plastic language utterly indifferent to the fortuitous appearance of things. But Cézanne, whatever he was, clearly was no philosopher, and his clumsy theorizing does not impress us today; the true basis of his yearning for fulfillment was a poetic temperament that in his water colors could be as tenderly lyrical as the verses of a Li Tai Po or, in his oils, as dramatic as King Lear.

To comprehend a Cézanne one must stand before it long after the spell of subject matter (of which there is little) has worn off. In time, the intensity and directness of the work burn through, and we forget we are in an exhibition room; instead, we are submerged in the picture and completely identified with the majesty of nature as projected through the tight telescoped space of Cézanne. To understand Cézanne, one must also read his countless expressions of dissatisfaction with himself, his endless complaints about not being able to "realize" his pictorial aims. Indeed, he was not easily satisfied. The dealer Ambroise Vollard sat one hundred and fifteen times for one portrait; when they had to part, Cézanne declared that he was not displeased with the front of the shirt. About two years before his death in 1906, when he had at last been acknowledged by the more progressive critics, and when he felt that he had managed to "realize" some of his goals, he wrote to the same Vollard:

"I am working obstinately. I am beginning to see the Promised Land. Shall I be like the great leader of the Hebrews or shall I be able to enter it? . . . I have made some progress. Why so late and with such difficulty? Is art indeed a priesthood which demands the pure in heart, completely dedicated to it?"

Though Gauguin and Van Gogh were, in their own ways, as dedicated as Cézanne, he utterly disliked Gauguin whom he accused of wanting to steal his formula, and he saw in Van Gogh's paintings the work of a madman. He could not understand why Gauguin had to go to the tropics to seek new subjects; he, Cézanne, found all the inspiration he needed in the roundness and full color of an apple; in a rare outburst of self-assertion, he once exclaimed, "With an apple I will astonish Paris!"

Cézanne, nine years older than Gauguin — who was born in Paris in 1848 — never saw any of the work the younger man produced in the South Seas. Had he seen it, he might have dismissed it as frivolous and sensational. To this very day, Gauguin has been misunderstood by many who regard him only as a man completely without a soul. In his middle years, he gave up his well-paying position as a stockbroker and subsequently left his family in order to pursue his artistic goals in Britanny, the West Indies, Arles, and finally in the South Seas. Yet in the many letters and journals he penned abroad, there is a repeated emphasis on the "soul" as the beginning and end of all painting, all life. Amid repetitive complaints about poverty, sickness, the treachery of dealers, and the hostility of critics, there was the genuine artist. Like Cézanne, but with greater articulateness, he often speculated on the aims of art, and his words contain the gist of the aesthetic philosophy of what, seven years after his death, became known as Post-Impressionism:

"In painting one must search rather for suggestion than for description, as is done in music."

"It is better to paint from memory, for thus your work will be your own: your sensation, your intelligence, and your soul will triumph over the eye of the amateur."

In the informal notes from Tahiti, known as his *Intimate Journals*, Gauguin wrote:

"Do not finish your work too much. An impression is not sufficiently durable for its first freshness to survive a belated search for infinite detail; in this way you let the lava grow cool and turn boiling blood into a stone. Though it were a ruby, fling it far from you."

Gauguin, who began as one of the lesser Impressionists, turned against the Impressionist movement (but not against his teacher Pissarro) years before his departure for the South Seas. "Their edifice rests upon no solid base . . . they heed only the eye and neglect the mysterious centers of thought." It is ironic that this man, whose alleged "materialism" has been decried so often, was actually the most ardent exponent of the anti-realistic, anti-materialistic, metaphysical trend that was to free art from the grossly academic contaminants of the nineteenth century. His detractors called his works "posters" because of the broad flat color area bounded by black outlines. To other observers, however, they have recalled the stained-glass windows of medieval cathedrals, sufficiently realistic and map-like to guide the onlooker into what the German poet Novalis called "the mysterious path that leads inward," but at the same time sufficiently abstract to prevent him from straying into seductive byroads.

Gauguin's work has lent itself to interpretations by many of his admirers. Among these was Albert Aurier, who hailed Gauguin as the chief of *symbolist* art. "Paul Gauguin," he wrote, "seems to me to be the initiator of a new art. The normal and final goal of painting, as of all arts, cannot be the direct presentation of objects. Its ultimate goal is to express Ideas by translating them into a special language. To the eyes of the artist, that is to the eyes of him who should be the one *who expresses absolute beings,* objects are valueless merely as objects. They can only appear to him as *signs.*"

Another term created in Gauguin's lifetime to describe his work was "Synthetism"; it referred to the use by Gauguin and his followers of broad, simple "synthetic" lines and colors different from the analytical realism of the Impressionists. *Cloisonnisme* (from the cloisonné enamel of the Middle Ages) was also used for Gauguin's (and subsequently Rouault's) style, since emphasis is given to forms in a picture by the surrounding deep, lead-like lines. Finally, Gauguin has been acclaimed, along with his friend Vincent van Gogh, a father of *Expressionism,* because he often distorted or exaggerated the ordinary forms and colors of nature in order to achieve emotional or aesthetic effects.

He was among the first to use color arbitrarily, and he did so "to convey the musical sensations that emanate from its very nature." To emphasize that the physical and the metaphysical were two different things, he crystallized his philosophy in these magnificent words: "I shut my eyes in order to see." To those who could not read his pictures, or needed further explanations, Gauguin insisted that he was not a painter after nature, that

Figure 4. Paul Gauguin:
The Moon and The Night.

Collection, The Museum
of Modern Art, New York.
Lillie P. Bliss Collection

15

everything sprang from imagination, that in the end he always dispensed with the model. Yet few of his contemporaries understood why he finally went to Tahiti, thousands of miles from Paris. He went there to seek rejuvenation — he was forty-seven when he embarked on his second and final trip to the South Seas — but not physical rejuvenation. He fled to the realm of the primitive in order to return to the purity of style, to the kind of anti-naturalistic art, with its perfect sense of simplified design, that was practiced in the Middle Ages.

Although neither Tahiti, nor Hiva-Oa in the Marquesas Islands where he died most miserably in 1903, was the untouched paradise he had hoped to find, modern art gained by this first contact of a truly modern man with the surviving remnants of Oceanic culture. Art, through Gauguin, again became simple, straightforward, and monumental, as though Giotto's frescoes had been painted southeast of Eden.

Gauguin and Vincent van Gogh were friends, after a fashion, but only for a short time. Van Gogh had been an employee of an art gallery, a schoolmaster in England, a clerk in a bookshop, and finally a lay preacher to miners in Belgium. He was thirty-five when, in February 1888, he left Paris for the city of Arles in Southern France. In October, Gauguin also went to Arles. The two high-strung, temperamental artists lived and worked together for two months. Then in a fit of madness, Van Gogh tried to kill Gauguin, who fled back to Paris. Two years and seven months later, at Auvers, a small town north of Paris, Vincent, dissatisfied, lonely, and fearing that his spells of insanity might become more frequent and last longer, shot himself.

Movies and sensational novels have popularized the tragic story of this ardent, self-taught Dutchman who groped for years for the path to truth that was finally revealed in a feast of blazing light. Vincent began by humbly copying the works of well-known artists, but eventually he produced those explosions of unbridled color that expressed not what he saw, but what he felt about the sun, the heat, the intrinsic beauty of persons and places. Many books have been written about him, but during his lifetime he received only one favorable review (by the critic Albert Aurier) and sold only one picture. The best guide to his "expressionist" work can be found in the hundreds of letters he wrote to his faithful brother Theo, to his family and to friends. Looking at his oils, few people now deplore the lack of academic accuracy and smooth technique that seemed so all-important to

Figure 5. Vincent van Gogh: Hospital Corridor at Saint Rémy.

Collection, The Museum of Modern Art, New York. Bequest of Mrs. John D. Rockefeller, Jr.

critics a generation ago: "So simple an object as a jug containing some flowers is drawn [by Van Gogh] with the uncouthness of the immature, even childish executant." What we now admire is Van Gogh's spontaneous boldness of color and design, unselfishly put to the service of suffering humanity. As the painter himself explained:

"In a picture I want to say something comforting as music is comforting. I want to paint men and women with something of the eternal which the halo used to symbolize, and which we seek to give by the actual radiance and vibration of our colorings . . ."

Intrinsically, Van Gogh's subject matter is neither troubling nor depressing: still lifes, Parisian and Provencal vistas, interiors, humble friends. Yet unlike his great admirer Matisse, who was a happy, well-balanced family man and was to reach a famous and secure old age, Vincent could not often "say something comforting," particularly not in his self-portraits, which reveal his unattractive features and behind them a turmoil of unrest and frustration. Nor did he always seek to "express hope by some star, the eagerness of a soul by a sunset radiance." He was fully aware of the "terrible passions of humanity," and in his celebrated *Night Café* (an ordinary provincial café in the city of Arles) he endeavored to express them "by means of red and green."

He called himself an "arbitrary colorist." Like Gauguin, he knew the symbol-creating power of the colors and used, particularly in his final years, strong, fervent pigments in agitated brush-strokes, not to please anybody, but to express a sincere human feeling. In the course of a few years, he got very far away from the Impressionists whom he had emulated for a while; although they sought to give views of the world around them with a more than photographic accuracy, Van Gogh became concerned with a truth higher and more profound than that. Even before he reached Paris he had written from his native Holland: "My great longing is to learn to make those very incorrections, those deviations, remodelings, changes of reality, that they may become, yes, untruth if you like — but more true than the literal truth."

He distinguished himself from the Impressionists by firmer drawing, sharper clarity of design, stronger contours, and large areas of flat, luminous color. Above all, he wanted to transfigure reality, whereas they contented themselves with merely describing it. From somber and unpromising provincial beginnings, his art finally reached a height of intensity, vitality, exuberance, and "significant form" that made it triumph soon after the maker himself had ceased to exist. Young Maurice Vlaminck, upon entering the Van Gogh Exhibition at Bernheim-Jeune's in Paris in 1901, exclaimed: "I love Van Gogh better than my own father." Of all the Fauves, Vlaminck came closest to Van Gogh.

Georges Seurat, born in 1859 and thus six years younger than Van Gogh, was not a tragic figure like the fiery, unbalanced Hollander. This rather uncommunicative man had friends who respected his great talent, and he had a companion who bore him a son. He was handsome, tall, well-balanced, of impeccable appearance. While Van Gogh's training as an artist came late and was rather spotty, the Parisian Seurat received a solid education and at the age of fifteen already had produced work that was highly competent. He was only a little over twenty when he moved away from the teachings of the Academy and with his systematic mind began to form what was to become the most original contribution to painting in the late nineteenth century. There was no apparent reason why he should not expect to reach a ripe old age. In March 1891 he helped arrange an exhibition of the Salon des Indépendants that showed some of his most recent works as well as paintings by Van Gogh, who had died less than a year earlier. Suddenly he was struck down by a fever, dying at the age of thirty-one. Pissarro, who, though nearly forty years older than Seurat, had become a follower of this young man, wrote to his son that while Seurat's "Pointillism" was finished, he

Figure 6. Georges-Pierre Seurat:
Fishing Fleet at Port-en-Bessin.

thought that it would "give rise to other effects which later will have great artistic significance." "Seurat," he added, "really brought something." Another "Pointillist," Paul Signac, slightly younger than Seurat, was to undertake the task of continuing the struggle for his friend's ideals; he confided to his diary: "Seurat gave everything he could give, and that admirably . . . his task was accomplished with finality. . . . What more can one ask of a painter?"

Seurat left hundreds of drawings, numerous small oil paintings, and five very large major paintings. Although the movement he initiated was called "Neo-Impressionism" and "Pointillism," Seurat himself preferred the term "Divisionism." Cézanne wanted to "make of Impressionism something solid and durable, like the art of the museums," because he was distressed by the softness and formlessness into which Monet and his associates had deteriorated, but Seurat resolutely turned away from Impressionism altogether. And while the Impressionists wanted to catch the fugitive aspects of their subject and to reveal faithfully "nature as seen through their temperaments," the scientifically-minded Seurat endeavored to subordinate his observations to a carefully wrought composition. In order to uncover what he believed to be the permanent qualities beneath the accidents of appearance, he — like Cézanne — dared to take liberties with reality. The Impressionists, of course, preceded him in using the method of applying paint in small spots of pure color not previously mixed on the palette, and by this method succeeded in getting the bright tones of sunlight. But they painted rapidly in the open rather than in the studio and forsook all other formal devices in order to record shorthand impressions of light striking on the surfaces of objects.

Seurat, however, after having made preliminary sketches from the motif, painted in his studio. Unlike the Impressionists whose brush strokes are of uneven sizes, with mathematical precision he put on the canvas dots of more or less equal size. For instance, instead of using green, which is a combination of blue and yellow, Seurat filled an area with adjacent blue dots and yellow dots to be mixed by the eye of the spectator. The mixture does occur, but the dots themselves give his pictures the texture of a mosaic. An "abstract" look is achieved by this laborious method, as disciplined and painstaking as the Impressionist method is spontaneously exuberant. This "abstract" quality is enhanced by the fact that all of Seurat's pictures are based upon a precise organization of people and objects that, while clearly recognizable, are reduced to verticals and horizontals.

As so often happens, Seurat's practice was more successful than his theories, and we look admiringly at the shimmering architecture of his works without desiring to know whether or not his theories were scientifically valid. While his followers, excepting Signac, were lesser men and therefore nearly forgotten, Seurat was a great artist. Today only the art historians know of Charles Angrand, Henri-Edmond Cross, Albert Dubois-Pillett, Maximilien Luce, Hippolyte Petitjean and Théo van Rysselberghe, to mention a few of the many who came under the influence of his theory. The general public knows them no more than it knows Gauguin's "pupils," such as Emile Bernard, Paul Serusier, Isak Meyer de Haan (an ex-manufacturer turned painter), Emile Schuffenecker and Armand Séguin.

Many additional names are mentioned in any substantial book on Post-Impressionism, but in a brief chapter strict selectivity must be exercised. One who cannot be omitted, however, is Odilon Redon who, though he belonged to the generation of the Impressionists was not an admirer of their practices. In fact he was, with Seurat and others, instrumental in the creation of the anti-Impressionist Society of Independents, and for a while even served as its vice-president.

His sensitive and subtle flower still lifes, though they are based on loving observation of nature, emerge from the territories of the dream. This artist, who was much admired by the

poet Mallarmé and who has been hailed by the Surrealists as one of their forerunners, is not widely known. The other-worldly poetry of his work cannot be perceived at a glance. He explained what he was after when he wrote:

"There are those who want to confine the art of painting to reproducing only what they see. Whoever remains within these narrow limits restricts himself to an inferior ideal. The great painters of the past have proved that the artist, once he has mastered his medium and found in Nature his means of expression, is genuinely free to take his subjects from history or the poets, or to seek it in his imagination."

Fantasy is also the forte of the Belgian painter of English and Flemish parentage, James Ensor (1860–1949), who soon abandoned Impressionism to find a style entirely his own. Ensor

spent most of his life in his native city of Ostend, where he lived as a recluse, and where he found his inspiration in Flemish carnivals and in the sea-shells, weird masks and outlandish bric-a-brac sold in his family's souvenir shop. But Ensor's imagination produced masks and marionettes stranger than anything the local craftsmen could fashion. He was in love with everything sensuous and theatrical. Though his great productive period was over by 1900, within a few years he had built fascinating pictures out of apparently disparate elements, distorting, exaggerating, inventing, and using strong, vibrant color. In practice he was very close to the general tenets of the Post-Impressionists, but he was not active in any of the major contemporary movements, and he was opposed to any trend in art that was based on an intellectual credo. "Reason is the enemy of art," he wrote, "All rules, all canons of art, vomit death."

Ensor was seriously concerned with the deterioration of European society, using religious themes to dramatize its short-comings. Though in Ensor's paintings there is little direct reference to the world conflagrations through which he lived — he even survived the second World War — he was aware of brutality and injustice, and his work is full of imaginative attacks against politicians, false educators, vivisectionists, alcoholics and others whom he loathed.

He shared a negation of theory as well as a sharply satirical eye with Henri de Toulouse-Lautrec (1864–1901). The dwarfed, amoral aristocrat Lautrec, however, portrayed with detachment the habitués of cafés, the prostitutes and drinkers, much as the Impressionists had described cathedrals and haystacks. He was close to none of the Impressionists except Edgar Degas, whom he admired greatly. Degas was very reluctant with a good word for any fellow-artist, but he encouraged the young, misshapen man in whom others saw only a brillant dilettante. "Well, Lautrec," he said, "I can see you're one of our trade." From Degas, who was never a true Impressionist, he learned to select aspects of reality that had never before been observed. His views seen from above, his technique of setting the main figure off-center in a scene, of giving the foreground unexpected importance in relation to the subject as a whole, these and other innovations, corresponding to what the camera can do, he got from Degas.

Lautrec's career was short. But his drawings and oils, immaculate in craftsmanship, full of feverish excitement and emotional tension, vastly expanded the frontiers of aesthetic experience by including people and scenes never to be found on the tame and almost bourgeois canvases of the Impressionists. He belonged to no group, and he exhibited only in the Salon des Indépendants.

26

Yet in his daring, in his dismissal of traditional taboos, he was one of the Moderns, and it is not astonishing that Rouault and Picasso willingly learned from him.

Among the Post-Impressionists are also two close friends, Pierre Bonnard (1867–1947) and Edouard Vuillard (1868–1940), who show a number of similarities to several of the artists already discussed. From Gauguin, no less than from the Japanese, Bonnard learned the use of flat color planes and simplified forms. The influence of Gauguin, Van Gogh, Redon, and Cézanne was clear in the revolutionary association of artists, the Nabis (from the Hebrew *nabi*, "prophet") that flourished in the 1890's and to which Bonnard and Vuillard belonged. The group's theoreti-

27

cian, Maurice Denis, summed up the Nabis' doctrine by emphasizing the Two Distortions: "The Objective Distortion, based upon a purely aesthetic and decorative concept, upon technical principles of color and composition, and the Subjective Distortion, which brought into play the artist's own perception . . ."

It was the same Maurice Denis who, as early as 1890, turned a sentence that might be construed as heralding the Age of Abstraction, though the first true Abstractions, the work of Vasily Kandinsky, were not to appear until about twenty years later:

"Remember that a picture — before being a battle horse, a nude woman, or some anecdote — is essentially a plane surface covered with colors assembled in a certain order."

Although the two friends had nothing to do with the Abstract Movement, which started about the time they had reached their peaks, something of the impersonal, detached and purely decorative that is seen in much of the non-objective, non-figurative paintings of the last thirty years, can be found in their work.

Figure 11. Maurice Denis:
Annunciation.
Rijksmuseum Kröller-Müller,
Otterlo

28

Figure 12. Édouard Vuillard:
Mother and Sister of the Artist.

Collection, The Museum
of Modern Art, New York.
Gift of Mrs. Saidie A. May

Bonnard's subject is often not unlike that of the Impressionists: landscapes, gardens with flowers, female nudes in interiors. But he does not aim at depicting all this with an Impressionist emphasis on the light that envelops everything. In his interiors everything seems to be woven into a tapestry-like pattern. When he shows people in a room, they are so integrated that they are part of the whole exactly as are the chairs, the table, and the wallpaper. There is no action, no anecdote in his serene pictures, and as a result they are more interesting for his unique feeling for surface and texture than for the subject matter. The same calmness prevails in the works of Vuillard, known for his sensi-

29

Figure 13. Henri Rousseau:
The Dream.

Collection, The Museum
of Modern Art, New York.
Gift of Nelson A. Rockefeller

30

Figure 14. Henri Rousseau:
The Wedding.
Mme. Jean Walter Collection, Paris

tive portraits and for his small interior scenes. Bonnard and Vuillard, on account of their quiet, restful indoor pictures, are often referred to as "Intimists."

Roger Fry, in the London exhibitions referred to earlier, also included one of the strangest figures to appear in the world of art, the entirely self-taught "primitive" Henri Rousseau. To distinguish him from several other French artists named Rousseau, his contemporaries dubbed him *Le Douanier*, though he was not a customs official but a minor toll-collector at a station on the outskirts of Paris. He has often been called the father of modern "Sunday painting," yet he was hardly a *peintre du Dimanche*. Between his retirement from service at the age of forty-one and his death in near-obscurity twenty-five years later, he worked assiduously day after day, challenging the public with the most unacademic oils France had ever seen.

He had some links with the Post-Impressionists insofar as he exhibited regularly at their Salon des Indépendants, and had of course met Gauguin, Van Gogh, Seurat, and Lautrec. It was Lautrec who defended the Douanier when some of the Indépendants wanted to expel the naive, middle-aged little painter because the public had strongly objected to his pictures. Lautrec won, and other unprejudiced artists and critics, although aware of Rousseau's technical shortcomings, found his paintings as enchanting as imaginative Japanese color prints or monumental Egyptian tomb paintings. In them there was the poetry of folk artists who never studied anatomy, never paused to compare the proportions of one subject with those of another, and could give uninhibited expression to their dreams.

Like many a primitive, Rousseau was happily unaware of his technical limitations. Basically he had that sense of "significant form" that Clive Bell and Roger Fry demanded from good artists, that innate feeling for composition that should precede any schooling or acquisition of skill. Being self-taught, he took nothing for granted; he had the untrammeled vision of a child freshly discovering the world and seeing details likely to be overlooked by the blasé intellectual.

Among his works there are numerous jungle scenes, yet he never left France, never saw the tropics (the story that as a youth, he went to Mexico as regimental musician in a French expeditionary corps no longer finds much credence). Instead, he made studies in the Paris zoological and botanical gardens and relied primarily on his vivid imagination. His exotic jungles are full of round-eyed animals which stare at us with the same intense astonishment that most of his human sitters betray.

With the other "Post-Impressionists" singled out for discussion in this volume, he shared the feeling for rhythm, the sensitivity to color relations, and the gift for simplification that are their main characteristics. Of these artists, all but two — the Hollander Van Gogh and the Belgian Ensor — were French. Other non-French painters of note who might be mentioned here are the melancholy Norwegian Edward Munch (1863–1944), who came to Paris in 1889 and for his nightmarish pictures de-

Figure 15. Edvard Munch:
The Dance of Life.
National Gallery, Oslo

rived a great deal of inspiration from Gauguin, Van Gogh and Toulouse-Lautrec; and the Swiss, Ferdinand Hodler (1853–1918) whose highly stylized, controlled landscapes, decorative and flat in color, have an affinity to the work of Cézanne and Seurat.

For Roger Fry, Post-Impressionism was a convenient term that also covered Matisse, Picasso, and others who had come to the fore after 1900. We do not include them here, for from the vantage point of the 1960's we were able to see other groups, such as the Fauves, Cubists, Futurists, Surrealists, and Expressionists, whose offerings were far "wilder" in technique and subject matter than even the most unorthodox pictures created by any one of these ten major Post-Impressionists discussed here. The Post-Impressionists have long ceased to be considered revolutionaries, but their work continues, through strength of form and freedom in imagination and color, to exert its virile charm upon the eyes of all sensitive humans.

Figure 16. Ferdinand Hodler:
The Grand Muveran.

The Art Institute of Chicago.
Helen Birch Bartlett
Memorial Collection

· 1 ·
CÉZANNE

Still Life with Peppermint Bottle

Painted 1890–1891
25⅜″ x 31⅞″
National Gallery of Art,
Washington, D.C.
Chester Dale Collection

Shy, boorish and pathologically afraid of humans, Cézanne seldom employed models. He rarely painted flowers because they withered away too quickly for so slow-working, methodical a painter. Yet he loved to arrange objects, such as bottles, glasses, and fruit. His aim was not so much to evoke the atmosphere of domesticity, as to express his feelings by means of the ordinary things which he put together with the wisdom of an architect, aware of the rhythmic order created through verticals and horizontals, through circles, ovals and cones.

Thus Cézanne employed the large, simple flask, and the narrower peppermint bottle, whose double curvature must have fascinated him; the brilliantly white napkin, and exciting curves of the heavy blue cloth; and finally the good, round apples. This dynamic group is set against a smooth background which is divided only by a few lines. White-gray-violet tones are dominant, and only a few red and yellow color accents are added as highlights to guide the eye along a very complex structure.

Cézanne painted still lifes throughout his long career, and as he moved closer to "abstraction," so his still lifes veered in this direction. Picasso, Braque and the other Cubists learned a great deal from Cézanne, intensifying their researches into the structure of objects beneath the surface, and their geometric relationships to one another.

· 2 ·
CÉZANNE

The Card Players

Painted 1890–1892
17¾″ x 22½″
Louvre, Paris,
galleries of the Jeu de Paume

Of Cézanne's five oil paintings of card players, one has five figures, another four, and the remaining, only two. In addition, several studies of single players have come down to us. The artist, who felt most uncomfortable in the presence of educated and rich people — though he had gone to good schools in his youth and, as the son of a banker, was not used to poverty — was at ease only with humble, unsophisticated people, such as his gardener Vallier or the Provençal farmers whom he watched in the small cafés in and around Aix.

In the last century, artists all over the world discovered what was called the "simple people," and they usually painted them with an exaggerated romantic sweetness. However, Cézanne attacked this theme with that ruthlessly direct realism that had been a tradition in France since the Le Nain brothers, in the early seventeenth century. Here, as elsewhere, he constructs the picture from volumes piled up with mathematical accuracy. The table, the chairs, the clothes are devoid of any decoration. The colors are subdued, and the drawing of the faces is reduced to a minimum, not allowing deep psychological penetration. Yet, despite the starkness and austerity, one feels that the artist was most sympathetic to these anonymous little people of the Provence, and in deep love with the theme. Thus he may be said to have felt these forms as grandiose elements, as visual sensations that acquire even greater meaning in the tight space into which they have been set.

· 3 ·

CÉZANNE

*Madame Cézanne in a
Yellow Chair*

Painted 1890–1894
31½″ x 25″
The Art Institute of Chicago

Hortense Fiquet was a simple, uneducated woman who served Cézanne as a model, bore him a son and finally, after many years of a difficult liaison with the unruly, undomesticated painter, became his wife in 1886. While Hortense was unable to appreciate Cézanne's work, she helped him a great deal by agreeing to pose for him whenever he so desired. At least a dozen portraits of her are in existence, and she is usually in frontal positions. In nearly all of the portraits she appears as a sullen, stolid figure who, to please the irascible Cézanne, had to sit as still as an apple. In reality she was an animated figure who loved to move around and talk a lot, but Cézanne forced her to sit silently in a rigid position for hours.

While the unfortunate woman appears exhausted, emptied out, as it were, by the numerous sittings such a portrait required, the picture itself is very much alive due to the fact that the artist infused each of the thousands of brush strokes with his own vitality, as he proceeded, here as elsewhere, with a conscientiousness that links him with the masters of the distant past. "The painter," he himself once said, "must rely on his vision. He must do everything according to nature with much reflection because every color-touch must contain air, light, the object, the plan, the character, the drawing, and the style; in a word, all that which constitutes a painting."

· 4 ·

CÉZANNE

La Montagne Sainte-Victoire

Painted in 1898
25½″ x 32″
The Baltimore Museum of Art
The Cone Collection

La Montagne Sainte-Victoire is a rugged limestone mountain, a little over 3,000 feet high, that rises abruptly from the undulating countryside east of Cézanne's native city of Aix. As a youth, he and his friends often climbed its clifflike slopes. When, in the middle of life, Cézanne recognized that Paris was not for him, and that he could only be completely himself and fully develop his talent in his native Provence, La Montagne Sainte-Victoire came to fascinate him to the point of obsession. During the last twenty-three years of his life, he repeatedly painted the mountain, or sketched it in water colors or oils. Whereas his earlier renderings of the scene are somewhat representational, here the artist has confined his interest to the contrast between the green bushes and pines, the orange stones in the foreground, and the truncated blue peak of the mountain in the background. This view is from the quarry of Bibèmus which supplied the yellow stone of which many houses in Aix were built.

Before 1900, few people outside Aix had ever heard of La Montagne Sainte-Victoire, which is not among the illustrious mountain peaks. It was Cézanne who put it on the map. Painting this mountain, which he could see clearly from his studio in the limpid Provençal air, the artist learned to "realize" his "sensation," to come close to his goal of making pictures as firm and lasting as those of the Old Masters. And yet Cézanne's aim was to create a new artistic world, diametrically opposed — at least in its tightly controlled forward-moving space — to traditional painting.

· 5 ·

CÉZANNE

Les Grandes Baigneuses

Painted 1898–1905
82″ x 98″
Philadelphia Museum of Art
W. P. Wilstach Collection

Like every artist, Cézanne made studies from the nude while still a student. Throughout his life he painted "Bathers" — a term used collectively for studies of nude figures. Cézanne's female nudes are totally different from those of his colleague Renoir. Whereas the latter was fond of women and much at ease in their presence, Cézanne was loath to employ a female model. Hence, in his "Bathers" he relied on schoolday drawings, old engravings, and even on the hasty notes he made while watching soldiers bathing in a stream near Aix. Thus, his stylized and even slightly deformed nudes, arranged in geometric groups, have little of the erotic seductiveness which is usually conjured up by the term "baigneuse." (According to his disciple and Boswell, Emile Bernard, Cézanne would have liked to use large groups of nudes and pose them on the banks of the local stream, but such a plan was impossible to carry out.)

Cézanne spent seven years on this particular composition, yet it remained unfinished. He was proud of it: "This will be my picture, my legacy to the world!" he said to a friend. The picture must be appreciated as a great essay in painterly architecture, with unclothed figures in a bluish landscape arranged to achieve the monumentality of a mural painting.

· 6 ·

GAUGUIN

The Schuffenecker Family

Painted in 1889
28¾″ x 36¼″
Louvre, Paris,
galleries of the Jeu de Paume

Emile Schuffenecker played an important role in Paul Gauguin's life. Gauguin met the small, dark-bearded Alsatian when he, Gauguin, joined a firm of stockbrokers in 1871. It was "Schuff," himself a minor painter, who persuaded the young stockbroker to visit those galleries that showed works of the moderns — the Impressionists. He also encouraged him to paint. Yet Gauguin took for granted all the acts of friendship which "Schuff" showered upon him, and so often abused the kindness of this man that "Schuff" finally broke with this egomaniac.

In this picture painted in 1889 — after Gauguin's return from Arles, and before his second stay in Brittany — the tension that existed between husband and wife, and finally led to a divorce, is subtly conveyed by the man's quizzical look at the woman whose expression appears to be sullen. Schuffenecker's shy, retiring manner is perfectly revealed. Note the Japanese print underneath the still life with fruit, probably one of Gauguin's paintings. The corner interrupting the blue wall is hardly noticeable, and the blue serves as a backdrop for the dramatis personae.

37

· 7 ·

GAUGUIN

Self-Portrait

Painted in 1889
31¼″ x 20¼″
National Gallery of Art,
Washington, D.C.
Chester Dale Collection

Of the many self-portraits Gauguin left, this one has more of the carica-ture about it. Poking fun at himself, the artist even put a halo above his head, as if to hint that he was a saint, or a prophet, of sorts. For he was the instigator for a new movement, Symbolism, that like everything new was bound to earn him the scorn and derision of the academicians and traditionalists. The term "Symbolism" was borrowed from the French poetry of his time and indicated that paintings should be symbols, the children of imagination, rather than merely painstaking records of ob-served facts. But Gauguin also used the term "Synthetism." Breaking with the principles he had derived from Impressionism, he came to use the broad, simple "synthetic" lines and color such as appear in this par-ticular picture. As one of his disciples, Maurice Denis, was to write, the Symbolists and Synthetists aimed at converting the emotions or spiritual conditions in the artist's imagination into equivalent signs and forms, "capable, if used in a painting, to create the same emotions or spiritual conditions in the observer without giving necessarily a reproduction of of the original optical impression."

· 8 ·

GAUGUIN

The Yellow Christ

Painted in 1889
36¼″ x 28⅞″
Albright-Knox Gallery,
Buffalo, N.Y.

High up in the Breton hills, near the southern coast of La Bretagne, is the hamlet Tremalo. Proof of the fact that Gauguin visited it during his stay at the nearby town of Pont-Aven is the striking similarity between the wooden crucifix in the 16th century chapel at Tremalo, and the figure of the *Yellow Christ*. This picture was painted in 1889, during the artist's second sojourn in Brittany, a rather backward part of France that offered quiet and peace to the harassed man, and also provided him with the "exotic" subject matter that could fertilize his imagination. Tired of Parisian sophistication and shallowness, Gauguin found "great rustic and superstitious simplicity" among the Bretons.

While the strong, gay colors are not to be found on the peninsula but come straight from the artist's exuberant soul, the landscape and the people are based on a reality that has not changed during the past seventy-odd years. Taking the cross out from the darkness of the little chapel into a field and placing three women, in their typical folk cos-tumes (still worn in the interior of Brittany) next to it, the mocker, the arch-bohemian created a picture lacking nothing in religious feeling. Yet *The Yellow Christ* has nothing in common with the thousands of genre pictures that have been produced in Brittany and elsewhere by fifth-rate painters slavishly reproducing what their eyes would see. Here, in this symphony of balanced colors and shapes, Gauguin demonstrated what he meant when, from Brittany he advised his friend Schuffenecker: "Don't copy nature too much," adding sagely: "Art is an abstraction; de-rive this abstraction from nature while dreaming in front of it, but think more of creating than of the actual result."

· 9 ·

GAUGUIN

The Spirit of the Dead Watching

Signed and dated:
P. Gauguin, '92
28⅝" x 36¾"
A. Conger Goodyear
Collection, N.Y.

Gauguin was among those rare artists who have left us in their writings numerous clues to their pictures. In a letter, mailed from Tahiti to his wife who, with her family, was staying in Copenhagen, the artist wrote, among other things: "I have made a nude of a young girl ... I put a little fear in her face. I must provide a pretext for the fear, if not explain it, and this must be in character with the girl, who is a Maori. These people traditionally fear the spirits of the dead ... The Kanakas [South Sea Islanders] think that the phosphorescent glows of night come from the spirits of the dead, they believe in them and fear them. Finally I have made the ghost just a plain little woman, for this girl, who has never seen French stage ghosts, can only picture the spirit of the dead as looking like the person who has died, in other words, a person like herself."

He also wrote at length about this picture to his friend, the painter Georges-Daniel de Monfried, explaining how he desired the imaginary flowers in the background to appear "at the same time (in the mind) like night phosphorences." Altogether, he was proud of this picture which, indeed, summarizes superbly the experiences of his first sojourn in the South Seas. When, on his return to Paris the following year, he put the painting up for sale at the Hotel Drouot in 1895, he was disappointed to note that it fetched less than half the amount he had hoped for.

· 10 ·

GAUGUIN

The White Horse

Signed and dated:
P. Gauguin, '98
62½" x 35¾"
Louvre, Paris,
galleries of the Jeu de Paume

What is the significance of this White Horse? (It is actually painted in a grayish-green, because the light shed upon it is filtered through the leafage above.) We do not know, and, perhaps, do not care to know. For we have moved into a world of fable, of mystery, in which this strange, riderless horse poses a question that is beyond answer.

Gauguin created this picture during his last and final stay in the South Seas. To him, 1898 was a particularly bad year; so bad, indeed, that he attempted suicide. Deep in debt, and physically ill, he obtained a clerical job in the capital of Tahiti, Papeete, though it drastically curtailed his time for creative work. Miraculously, these troubles and tribulations leave no trace in a work like this: calm, serene, and showing the painter at the peak of his artistic power. Nowhere is the liberating power of art more strongly proven than it is by this indisputable masterwork which has used an everyday theme as a pretext for an aesthetic experience of balanced colors and rythmically related linear patterns.

· 11 ·

VAN GOGH

Portrait of the Painter Bock

Painted in 1888
23½″ x 17⅞″
Louvre, Paris,
galleries of the Jeu de Paume

In several letters, Vincent van Gogh discussed this picture so completely that excerpts will be the viewer's best guide towards understanding:

"I want to put my appreciation, the love I have for him, into the picture. . . . I am now going to be the arbitrary colorist. I exaggerate the fairness of the hair. I even get to orange tones, chromes and pale citron-yellow.

"Behind the head, instead of painting the ordinary wall of the mean room, I paint infinity, a plain background of the richest, intensest blue that I can contrive, and by this simple combination of the bright head against the rich blue background, I get a mysterious effect, like a star in the depth of an azure sky."

Although Bock was actually a painter, Van Gogh, in a subsequent letter, wrote:

" . . . thanks to him I at last have a first sketch of that picture which I have dreamt of for so long — the poet. He posed for me. His fine head with that keen gaze stands out in my portrait against a starry sky of deep ultramarine; for clothes, a short yellow coat, a collar of unbleached linen, and a spotted tie . . ."

· 12 ·

VAN GOGH

Night Café

Painted September, 1888
27½″ x 35″
Yale University Art Gallery
Bequest of Stephen C. Clark

Painted a few days or weeks before the *Bedroom*, this picture is very different in mood. To his colleague, Emile Bernard, he thus described the café: "It is a café where night prowlers cease to be night prowlers, because they flop down at a table and spend the whole night thus without prowling at all." To his brother he wrote: "I have tried to express the terrible passions of humanity by means of red and green." This provincial café in Arles, on Place Lamartine, which still stands, is devoid of any particular dramatic features, yet the artist's unhappy soul endowed with gloom the few unsuspecting characters and the furniture, walls and installations (mark the light, radiating from the oil lamps in a symbolic fashion!). Van Gogh went further in his explanations:

"I have tried, as it were, to express the powers of darkness in a low drinking-shop, by soft Louis XV green and malachite, contrasting with yellow green and hard blue greens, and all this in an atmosphere like a devil's furnace, of pale sulphur."

Shortly before painting this picture, Van Gogh had asserted that he was determined to become an "arbitrary colorist," that is to say, he wanted to use colors for their expressive values rather than make faithful replicas of the images received by the eye. In this picture, he completely achieved his goal.

· 13 ·

VAN GOGH

The Bedroom at Arles

Painted October, 1888
28½″ x 36″
The Art Institute of Chicago
Helen Birch Bartlett
Memorial Collection

Van Gogh painted this interior twice — another version is in his nephew's collection at Laren, Holland. At Arles he rented one half of a two-story house (no longer standing) on the Place Lamartine, a house with a yellow exterior, known to us from the artist's paintings as the "Yellow House." Van Gogh at last had a sufficiently large apartment of his own, and he was particularly pleased with his comfortable bedroom where, in addition to the bed, he had a small table and two chairs. To his brother Theo he wrote about this picture:

"Color alone has to put the thing across, its simplification imparting a grander style to the work and hinting at rest and sleep generally. The sight of this picture is meant to relax the mind, or rather the imagination."

This deep-felt desire for plastic, as well as physical, harmony and well-being is reminiscent of what was to be written, several decades later, by a much happier, better integrated individual, the painter Henri Matisse, who expressed his goal in similar terms:

"What I dream of is an art of balance, of purity and serenity devoid of troubling or depressing subject matter, an art which might be for every mental worker . . . like an appeasing influence, like a mental soother, something like a good armchair in which to rest from physical fatigue."

The Bedroom in Arles is one of Van Gogh's most successful constructions by means of color, and one of mankind's favorite pictures.

· 14 ·

VAN GOGH

Self-Portrait

Painted in 1890
25½″ x 21¼″
Louvre, Paris,
galleries of the Jeu de Paume

Van Gogh has left us more than forty self-portraits. Like his spiritual ancestor, Rembrandt, he loved to scrutinize his own features which — like those of the seventeenth century artist — might be considered "unattractive," as they do not fit into the preferred patterns. But he also resorted to the self-portrait as a way out of a dilemma — he could not get any models: "Several people would ask me for portraits if they dared, but everyone is afraid of me."

This is his last self-portrait; a few weeks after having completed it, he was to fire the fatal bullet into himself. Yet it is hard to see in this picture any desire, on the artist's part, to "give up." The piercing glance of the eyes is as determined, as intense, as before. At the same time, there is something clearly pathological about the way the eyes thrust forward in what was Vincent's last self examination in glowing paint.

This picture must have had a special meaning for Van Gogh, for it was the only one he did not send to his brother Theo, but kept and himself brought to his physician, the alienist Dr. Gachet, a clever man who accepted from his hitherto unrecognized patient pictures in lieu of money. In this whirlpool of undulating long strokes, only a few touches of red in the beard relieve the uncanny green-bluishness of the canvas.

· 15 ·

VAN GOGH

The Church at Auvers

Painted in 1890
36½″ x 29½″
Louvre, Paris,
galleries of the Jeu de Paume

The little town of Auvers-sur-Oise, near Paris, was the last station in Van Gogh's troubled life. There he spent the late weeks of the spring, and the early weeks of the summer of 1890. One evening, in a field just outside Auvers, he shot himself. He died at Auvers two days after the shooting, attended by his faithful brother.

It has been written that "Vincent's work in Auvers-sur-Oise was only a last guttering of the candle before it was finally extinguished." What an extraordinary guttering it was to produce pictures like *The Town Hall at Auvers on Bastille Day,* or the present picture, in which rather ordinary edifices, with nondescript façades, are endowed with immortality by the vigorous and fervent brush of Vincent! While his color harmonies had grown cooler — after all, he was now no longer in the Provence, but under the northern sky of the Isle de France — there was greater life in his paintings, in which everything seems to be moving. At Auvers, his work became even more personal, more "stylized" to the point of being abstract. It makes no sense to speculate whether, by 1890, Van Gogh had spent all his energies, or whether, had the physicians been able to save his life, he might have painted pictures even greater than this one. All that can be said for sure is that in his brief stay at Auvers, the thirty-seven year old sick man enriched the world with masterpieces that, after many decades, have not lost their spell upon the beholder.

· 16 ·

SEURAT

A Sunday Afternoon on the Island of La Grande Jatte

Painted 1884–1886
78″ x 118″
The Art Institute of Chicago
Helen Birch Bartlett
Memorial Collection

La Grande Jatte is a long narrow island in the Seine River, beyond Neuilly. Today, all of it, save for the southernmost tip, is covered with small factories and repair shops, while the tip, a pleasure ground until World War II, is now being converted to a sports field. Happily, the tall trees which fascinated Seurat, will be preserved.

Unlike Monet, who usually spent no more than a few hours to catch on canvas nature's most fugitive aspects, Seurat spent many months on the project of portraying Sunday strollers and picnickers in relaxed positions and holiday moods. He made countless trips to the island, and by the time he had put the finishing touches to *Dimanche Après-Midi A L'Ile de la Grande Jatte,* as the French title runs, he had completed more than fifty preparatory drawings and paintings, some fairly large.

Like all of his major works, this one too is organized on vertical and horizontal lines, and he used dots of pure primary colors exclusively in accordance with the logical, almost scientific system popularly called "Pointillism." It has been charged that the painting was still and lifeless, and that the figures were doll-like, even inhuman. Others have found, however, that the huge picture exudes the "joy of living," characteristic of *La Belle Epoque,* and that what Seurat has given us here is a kind of architecturally conceived Garden of Eden.

· 17 ·

SEURAT

La Parade

Painted 1887–1888
39½″ x 59¼″
Metropolitan Museum of Art
Bequest of Stephen C. Clark

After Seurat's death, a critic wrote that his composition of figures were "obviously provisional attempts, first essays to apply step-by-step methods that are still vague." He continued by saying: "No doubt . . . that in due time Seurat would have managed to remove from his figures that rigid and congealed appearance which often prevents us from appreciating the authoritative purity of his draftsmanship."

Though we do not believe that Seurat's works are merely stepping-stones towards a goal that only death prevented the artist from reaching, it must be admitted that the terms "rigid" and "congealed" might be applied to *La Parade*, this daring combination of immobile figures — a row of cornet and trombone players at a fair, and, beneath it, the heads of spectators — in which the colors are more subtle, more subdued than in other works of his. The work, however, has often been praised chiefly as an exercise in rendering artificial light — the curious effects of the newly invented gas light. But while this painting is kept in a minor key, there is a variety of tones — violets and greys, deep blues, faint oranges and others — that, along with the silhouetted figures, help create a mysteriously poetic mood.

· 18 ·

SEURAT

Le Chahut

Painted 1889–1890
66″ x 55″
Rijksmuseum Kroller-Muller
Otterlo, The Netherlands

In his earlier paintings Seurat appeared preoccupied with the harmony of static scenes; here the emphasis is on movement. He did not, of course, paint this picture in any of the dancing halls or cabarets of Montmartre, where high-kicking performances were the fad at the end of the nineteenth century; he made pencil sketches on little cards he could hold in the palm of his left hand, and then painted the whole composition in the seclusion of his studio. As in *Le Cirque*, we have here a pyramid-like organization of moving figures under artificial lighting. One is reminded of Toulouse-Lautrec — but for a brief second only. For whereas Lautrec was a chronicler of the gay life of the French capital, and interested in the psychology of its celebrated entertainers, Seurat's dancers seem quite impersonal, de-individualized, and the only satirical touch is found in the delighted look of the top-hatted guest in the picture's lower right corner. Yet the picture is dominated by an exciting movement — the tension-producing swing, in unison, of the ballet-skirts.

SEURAT

Le Cirque

Painted 1890–1891
75″ x 60″
Louvre, Paris,
galleries of the Jeu de Paume

This is the last of Seurat's five large masterpieces. Here, the structural design is as carefully worked out as in *La Grande Jatte* and other works, yet there is far more animation. A dynamic figure is the clown, red-winged and white-masked, who opens the circus scene, as it were, and intoxicating movement is produced by the light, gay equestrienne whose foot is barely touching the galloping white horse. The expressions on the faces of the seated spectators are clearly marked, and there is none of the anonymity that characterized the Sunday folk on the Ile de la Grande Jatte. Exciting, too, is the color — flaming oranges, burning yellows and soft blues.

Le Cirque indicated that Seurat was moving into a new direction. Unfortunately, he did not have much longer to live — he was dead about a year after the picture was first exhibited in the Salon of the Indépendants, where its novelty of approach caused more amused or angry shaking of heads than expression of unmitigated admiration. The great painter Puvis de Chavannes, to Seurat's bitter disappointment, barely glanced at the picture, and then moved on. A memorial exhibition, held in Paris in 1892, roused little interest, and there were no sales. It was only in our century that Seurat was recognized as one, who, at the height of Impressionist fervor, deliberately turned away from the docile submission to nature and became one of the great forerunners of modern art.

· 20 ·

REDON

Bouquet of Flowers

Painted before 1875
10½″ x 7½″
Louvre, Paris,
galleries of the Jeu de Paume

Flower paintings existed in antiquity — in Egypt, and in Greece (where one man made his name as a painter of flowers). Flowers again appear in pictures made in the late Middle Ages, and they became a favorite subject particularly in the Low Countries, where several members of the Brueghel family excelled in this genre.

In modern times, the Impressionists and Post-Impressionists (Manet, Degas, Monet, Pissarro, Renoir, Gauguin, Van Gogh, to name a few) often painted flowers with delight and gusto. In the work of Odilon Redon — oils, water colors, pastels, drawing and prints — flowers in vases play a major role. Their variety in color, pattern, shape, fascinated him. Besides, they were the most poetic, most mysterious things his eyes could dwell upon. Redon studied nature most carefully (his friendship with the botanist Armand Clavaud taught him much about the world of nature), yet his work is high above the timid Naturalism that attempts exact replicas of nature's creations. In his writings he emphasized: "While I recognize the necessity for a basis of observed reality ... true art lies in a reality that is *felt*" (italics mine). In a subtle, unobtrusive way, he transformed and transfigured nature. What he presents us with is the essence, the poetry of flowers rather than their botanical characteristics. Above all, he had the gift to orchestrate these flowers into striking harmonies of an uncanny beauty. To quote him once again: "All my originality consists in the fact ... that I put, as far as possible, the logic of the visible at the service of the invisible."

ENSOR

The Entry of Christ into Brussels

Painted in 1888
101½" x 169½"
Royal Museums of Fine Arts,
Antwerp

The Belgian James Ensor was realist and surrealist in one, physical and metaphysical. It is a matter of record that by 1900 he had anticipated quite a few of twentieth century trends in art such as Fauvism, Expressionism, Dubuffet's *art brut*, and even the abstract expressionism of the 1950's. So much was he in advance of his times that in 1889 the most progressive of artists' associations in Brussels refused to show his gigantic proto-expressionist *Entry of Christ into Brussels*, and almost succeeded in expelling him from the organization (he escaped expulsion by only one vote — his own).

Ensor had the reputation of being anti-religious, yet the figure of Christ turns up repeatedly in his work. He himself, with his ascetic face, long hair and beard, somewhat recalled the traditional image of Christ, and he even represented himself as Christ, mocked by the people, since he considered himself misunderstood and maltreated by his contemporaries. When he worked on the *Entry of Christ*, he was in straitened circumstances, found it difficult to obtain the necessary pigments, and to complete this huge canvas — more than fourteen square yards! — in the narrow space of his studio. It was rolled up for a long time, and framed only in 1920, when, for the first time, it was sent to an exhibition.

Painted in a loose, almost hasty manner, this picture shows Christ, a tiny, wide-haloed figure on a donkey, completely lost in a crowd of leering, ugly, masklike faces, dwarfed by standards, banners, and pennants (one streamer proclaims, "Vive la Sociale" — Long live the Social State!). This masterwork may remind one of a famous painting by a spiritual ancestor of this modern artist — *Christ Carrying the Cross,* by Pieter Brueghel the Elder. There, too, the people wear contemporary — in this case, sixteenth century — dress, and there, too, it takes time to discover, among the antlike creatures around Him, the tiny figure of Christ. But whereas in the times of Brueghel, or Bosch, pictures of this sort were no rarity, Ensor painted his *Entry* when it was an "anachronism." For the Impressionist era did not produce social manifestoes using religious themes to satirize a decadent society. Curiously, when the picture was again shown in the "Fifty Years of Modern Art" exhibition at the Brussels World's Fair of 1958, the public, used to abstractions sans message or theme, looked at this painting as if it were by a medieval Fleming, and not by a master who lived until the year 1949.

· 22 ·

TOULOUSE-LAUTREC

At the Moulin Rouge

Painted in 1892
47¼″ x 55″
The Art Institute of Chicago

For many years after it opened in 1889 the Moulin Rouge ("Red Mill"), at the corner of the Place Blanche and rue Lepic, was the most famous dance hall of Montmartre. For a while it was the most celebrated pleasure resort of tourists, thanks, to a large extent, to the dancer, La Goulue, who appears in many of the paintings of one habitué, the dwarfed and crippled aristocrat, Henri Toulouse-Lautrec.

In this particular painting, however, La Goulue, for a change, appears in the background only (her arms raised, she is arranging her hair in front of a mirror). The two men standing in the background are the heavily bearded, tiny artist and, beside him, his regular companion, his cousin Gabriel Tapié de Céleyran. Seated in the foreground are several of his friends, among them the literary and music critic, Edouard Dujardin (with a yellow beard) and next to him, La Macarona, a Spanish dancer. To the right, lighted from below, is the masklike face of a certain Mlle. Nelly C., cut off by the frame. The composition, in its boldness — the illusion of space is made by the converging diagonals of floor boards and balustrade — reveals how much Toulouse-Lautrec had profited from studying his idol, Degas, as well as Japanese posters.

· 23 ·

BONNARD

Woman at the Breakfast Table

24″ x 27½″
Painted between 1905 and 1910
Kunsthaus, Zurich

Although Pierre Bonnard for a while belonged to a group who called themselves Nabis (the Hebrew for Prophets) and were greatly influenced by Gauguin, he actually never adhered to any particular aesthetic theory. He painted — to make use of Monet's simile — "as a bird sings," and he was not ashamed of telling his friend Matisse that basically he, Bonnard, was an Impressionist, though by that time Impressionism had long run its course. Undoubtedly, he had studied Japanese color prints and from them learned the use of flat planes and the reduction of modeling (by means of light and shade) to a bare minimum. But he never allowed theories to restrain his temperament, and while, in many respects, he was a Post-Impressionist, he was also an heir to Renoir and, through him, linked with the great French tradition, with Fragonard, with Watteau.

Bonnard, who lived an almost cloudless, uneventful life, surviving all those who had started out with him around 1890 and reaching the ripe age of eighty, did not need any unusual subject matter to excite his lust for painting. His wife Marthe, their dog Dingo and a table covered with dishes and fruit, served him repeatedly as a *sujet*. He himself once observed: "A painting is a series of spots which are joined together and ultimately form the object, the unit over which the eye wanders without obstruction." His joy in light and color made it possible for him to transform into a veritable gem even the most humble domestic scene. Yet he did not simply submit to the subject matter as it offered itself to the eye — he chose an interesting angle, perhaps under the influence of Degas. The freshness of color, the lyricism of approach, the charm of the texture make an otherwise banal theme most delightful to the eye. Bonnard once said: "I'm perfectly happy." This picture persuades us that he told the full truth.

· 24 ·

ROUSSEAU

War

Painted 1894.
Signed: Henri Rousseau
44½″ x 75.9″
Louvre, Paris,
galleries of the Jeu de Paume

Rousseau, who had served in the French army between 1864 and 1868, and again in the Franco-Prussian war of 1870/1871, loathed warfare. He once asked the German dealer and critic, Wilhelm Uhde: "Are you for peace?" Having been reassured on this point, the Douanier (customs inspector) lifted his glass in a toast. To Uhde he also made one of his few comments on topics outside of art: "If a king tries to start a war, a mother should go to him and forbid it."

This very large work is now in the center of one of the walls of the "Salle Gauguin," faced, on the opposite wall, by Rousseau's own *Snake Charmer* (Musée du Jeu de Paume). Its full title is: "War, or The Ride of Discord." There also exists a lithograph on red paper entitled, *The Horrors of War* (the only print Rousseau ever made), closely resembling the painting; it was reproduced in 1895 in the second issue of the short-lived review, *L'Ymagier,* edited by Alfred Jarry, and Rémy de Goncourt. For the catalogue of the Salon des Indépendants, where the picture was shown in 1894, Rousseau offered this explanation: "Frightful, she passes, leaving in her wake despair, tears, and ruins." Mysteriously, *War* disappeared shortly after the showing and was rediscovered in a cellar fifty years later.

As the sword-brandishing savage woman (*La Guerre*) on the black horse rushes forward, she leaves human corpses on the ground (the man in the center is identifiable as the painter himself). It has been argued that, in painting this picture, Rousseau may have been influenced by his friend Paul Gauguin (who used flat colors in simplified patterns), and by works of Uccello, Baron Gros and Delacroix. The coloring of the sky may suggest reflections of fires of war, or may simply indicate a sunset. Though "naive" in composition and certain details, this is as starkly apocalyptic a picture as is Picasso's *Guernica.*

THE COLOR SLIDE BOOK OF THE WORLD'S ART

Titles in this series

IMPRESSIONIST PAINTING
by ALBERT CHATELET, *Director of the Lille Museum*

DUTCH PAINTING OF THE 17TH CENTURY
by EMIL R. MEIJER, *Director of Educational Services*
of the Rijksmuseum, Amsterdam

THE HIGH RENAISSANCE — ITALIAN PAINTING
by EVELINA BOREA, *University of Bologna*

EARLY FLEMISH PAINTING
by ROBERT L. DELEVOY, *Professor, Institute of Art and Archaeology, Brussels*

PAINTING BY THE POST-IMPRESSIONISTS
by ALFRED WERNER, *Contributing Editor, "Arts Magazine"*

other titles in preparation

EARLY ITALIAN PAINTING

ENGLISH PAINTING 1740–1850

EARLY GERMAN PAINTING

SPANISH PAINTING — THE GOLDEN CENTURY